Act Like Somebody

A Collection of Moments of Parenting from *The Andy Griffith Show*

Compiled by Ken Beck and Jim Clark

RUTLEDGE HILL PRESS™ • NASHVILLE, TENNESSEE
A DIVISION OF THOMAS NELSON, INC.
www.ThomasNelson.com

Dedicated to our parents:
Hazel and Al Beck
Nancy and Blake Clark

Additional material and compilation copyright © 2002 Ken Beck & Jim Clark

Published by Rutledge Hill Press, a Thomas Nelson company,
P.O. Box 141000, Nashville, Tennessee 37214.

Design by OneWomanShow Design, Franklin, TN.

Photographs on pages 8 and 17 are courtesy of Bart Boatwright Collection.
Photographs on pages 12 and 36 are courtesy of Gilmore-Schwenke Archives.
Photograph on back endsheet is courtesy of Steve Cox Collection.

Library of Congress Cataloging-in-Publication Data

Act like somebody: a collection of moments of parenting from the Andy Griffith show / compiled by Ken Beck and Jim Clark.
    p. cm.
  ISBN 1-55853-995-6 (hardcover)
  1. Andy Griffith show (Television program) I. Beck, Ken, 1951- II.
Clark, Jim, 1960-
  PN1992.77.A573 C65 2002
  791. 45'72--dc21

                         2002003736

Printed in the United States of America

02 03 04 05 06—5 4 3 2 1

Acknowledgments

We had invaluable assistance from many people in putting together this book. At Rutledge Hill Press, publisher Larry Stone nurtured the idea of this book, editor Geoff Stone then treated it with kid gloves, and marketing man Bryan Curtis and all of the staff at Rutledge Hill have been there to help it grow to full maturity.

We also thank designer Angie Jones. Her work with the pictures and other graphics has made the words have even greater beauty and impact. We're likewise grateful to Allan Newsome for his valuable help.

We thank everyone at Paramount and parent company Viacom for their efforts in licensing and overseeing this book. We especially wish to acknowledge the work of Risa Kessler and Phyllis Ungerleider.

For their help in gathering photographs, we thank Jason Gilmore and Jim Schwenke of Gilmore-Schwenke Archives, Bart Boatwright, Steve Cox, and TAGSRWC Archives. Thanks also to Jack Ginn for his input. And we thank all of the actors whom we've enjoyed watching as they have spoken the unforgettable words that are included in these pages.

But it is for the words themselves that this book owes most of its debt. This book is a tribute to the amazing group of incredibly talented writers who worked on *The Andy Griffith Show*. For more than forty years, we have been in ever-increasing awe of their abilities every time we watch an episode. Credits for their words accompany the excerpts of each episode's dialogue used in the book.

Ken also thanks his fellow parent and wife, Wendy, and their daughter Kylie and son Cole. Jim thanks his wife, Mary.

And we thank the person without whom there simply could be no book about parenting in Mayberry: the Father Figure of Mayberry and of the show itself, Andy Griffith.

Introduction

From the standpoint of ongoing storytelling, having Andy Taylor be a single parent raising his young son was a brilliant stroke by the creators of The Andy Griffith Show. Doing so allowed for Andy's character to be involved in all kinds of interesting storylines about dating and other adventures, while also keeping the show from being a typical domestic situation comedy.

It's hard to take a snapshot of Andy and Opie's relationship with just one or two lines here and there. Many of their best moments together are the extended father-and-son talks that they have through the years. The book is organized chronologically to provide a view of how Andy and Opie's relationship evolves as Opie grows up and new issues of parenting arise.

And, naturally, with parenting experts like Barney Fife around, there's always plenty of unsolicited advice available to Andy about how to raise his boy. Plus there are interesting and sometimes helpful ideas about parenting from folks such as Goober, Floyd, and of course Aunt Bee.

The goal of The Andy Griffith Show was simply to create half-hour episodes of outstanding entertainment. But because of the great care involved with all aspects of the show's production, moments of parental wisdom and love couldn't help but shine through as a natural part of the show's thoughtful storytelling. This book tries to capture some of the best of these moments. As an extension of Mayberry's parenting, some of the proceeds from this book are being donated to Court Appointed Special Advocates (CASA), a group that assists children in the judicial system.

—K.B. and J.C.

ANDY: All ready for school, are you?

OPIE: Yes.

ANDY: Well, do a good day's work and *act like somebody.*

"Barney's Replacement," Episode 34
Written by Jack Elinson and Charles Stewart

With Opie seemingly unconvinced that Aunt Bee would be any good at raising him, Aunt Bee decides that he'd be better off if she didn't stay. Of course, even if Aunt Bee may not have the skills to raise Opie, maybe there's another good reason for her to stick with Opie:

OPIE: Don't go, Aunt Bee! I don't want you to. I want you to stay.

AUNT BEE: You do?

ANDY: You mean it, Opie?

OPIE: Sure.

ANDY: Well, what changed your mind?

OPIE: Well, if she goes, what'll happen to her? She doesn't know how to do anything—play ball, catch fish, or hunt frogs. She'll be helpless.

ANDY: Well, yeah, I guess that's right. A woman that don't know how to do important things like that—why, she'd just be lost.

OPIE: So that's why she's gotta stay, so I can teach 'em to her.

You need me!

"The New Housekeeper," Episode 1
Written by Jack Elinson and Charles Stewart

When Opie gives only three cents to the underprivileged children's charity, Andy tries to explain to him about the worthiness of the cause and the need to give more:

ANDY: Now, look here. We better talk about this thing. Now, look here, Opie, you can't give a little bitty piddlin' amount like three cents to a worthy cause like the underprivileged children's drive. I was readin' here just the other day where there's somewhere like four hundred needy boys in this county alone. Or one and a half boys per every square mile.

OPIE: There is?

ANDY: There sure is.

OPIE: I never seen one.

ANDY: Never seen one what?

OPIE: A half a boy.

ANDY: Well, it's not really a half a boy. It's a ratio.

OPIE: Horatio who?

ANDY: Not *Ho*ratio. A ratio. It's mathematics. 'Rithemetic. Look now, Opie. Forget that part of it. Forget the part about the half a boy.

OPIE: It's pretty hard to forget a thing like that, Pa.

ANDY: Well, try!

OPIE: Poor Horatio.

ANDY: Now look, Opie, Horatio is not the only needy boy … Son, didn't you ever give anybody anything just for the pleasure of it, something you didn't want anything in return for?

OPIE: Sure. Just yesterday I gave my friend Jimmy something.

ANDY: Now, that's fine! What did you give him?

OPIE: A sock in the head.

ANDY: I meant charity.

OPIE: I didn't charge him nothin'.

ANDY: I meant something for the joy of giving.

OPIE: I enjoyed it!

"Opie's Charity," Episode 8
Written by Arthur Stander

When Opie tells Andy that he traded his new cap pistol for what turned out to be phony licorice seeds and that he now plans to trade the licorice seeds to another friend for roller skates, Andy has to set him straight:

ANDY: Let me tell you something here. You know that you've been taught the Golden Rule: Do unto others as you'd have them do unto you?

OPIE: Yes, Pa.

ANDY: You think you've been following that rule?

OPIE: Sure. Tommy did unto me and now I'm doing it unto Jerry.

ANDY: Uh, I believe you're bending that rule just a little bit. Now the Golden Rule says that you're supposed to be honest and square-dealin' with other folks. Now, telling your friend that them seeds is gonna grow licorice sticks, well, that's kind of far away from what you'd call square-dealin' and it's awful close to what you'd call cheatin'.

OPIE: I didn't tell him that they'd grow licorice sticks, Pa. I just didn't tell him they wouldn't. Well . . . *I* got cheated.

ANDY: Well, now that still don't make it right. And I know you wouldn't feel good cheatin' your friend. Now, I tell you what to do. Now, you just keep them licorice seeds and forget this whole trade until you got something worthwhile to dicker with. All right?

(Opie nods.)

ANDY: All right. Now just always remember,

honesty is the best policy.

(Andy and Barney exit.)

OPIE (to self): If honesty is such a good policy, how come I'm out a cap pistol?

"The Horse Traders," Episode 14
Written by Jack Elinson and Charles Stewart

When Aunt Bee prepares to leave Andy and Opie home alone for a few days while she takes care of another relative who's ailing, she is concerned about whether Andy and Opie will be able to take care of themselves in her absence. But she finally pulls herself away, and Andy and Opie begin to fend for themselves:

OPIE: Boy, she sure does go on, don't she, Pa?

ANDY: Well, that's because she loves us, Opie, and she worries about us and wanting us to be healthy and comfortable and well taken care of.

OPIE: Yeah, but it sure is gonna be nice to be a messer-upper again for a couple of days.

ANDY: No you ain't and no I ain't. Come on. No sir, we're gonna be nice and neat and orderly—just like Aunt Bee wants us to be.

OPIE: We are?

ANDY: Yes sir. And we're gonna start right here in the kitchen and wash those dishes just like I promised Aunt Bee.

OPIE: Why? She ain't gonna be here to yell at us.

ANDY: Well now, you're a-lookin' at it wrong. See, that's like sayin' you milk a cow to get strong fingers. That's the wrong way to look at it. We ain't gonna be nice and neat and orderly to please Aunt Bee.

We're gonna be nice and neat and orderly because that's the right way to do things.

"Andy and Opie, Housekeepers," Episode 23
Written by David Adler (Frank Tarloff)

When Barney finds out that Opie has been having his milk money extorted from him by a bully, he reports the news to Andy:

BARNEY: It's just plain extortion's what it is!

ANDY: Well, that'd explain it, wouldn't it? He's too scared not to give him the nickel and too ashamed to tell me about it.

BARNEY: Why don't I go to that boy's home and tell his daddy?

ANDY: No, no. I know how you feel and that'd settle it for now. But what happens next time somebody goes pushing Opie around? Do you and me run in and solve it for him?

BARNEY: Well, Andy, he's scared...I mean, the other boy's so much tougher. Why don't I give Opie some lessons—a little jab-jab and chop-chop?

ANDY: Naw, naw, Barney. It's not lessons in fighting he needs. I just don't want him to be afraid. I don't want him to be the kind of boy that goes around looking for fights, but I just don't want him to run from one when he's in the right.

And the way that Andy figures out appropriately comes while he's fishing with Opie. He tells Opie the story about how the spot where they just fished was Andy's secret spot when he was a boy, but that bully Hodie Snitch followed him there one time and took Andy's spot away from him under the threat of a punch in the nose. Andy tells Opie how ashamed he was for not protecting what was rightfully his. Then he tells about something he learned along the way:

ANDY: **It's fine and dandy to give away something because you want to, but not because you're scared the other fella's gonna give you a punch in the nose if you don't.**

Andy continues his story by telling Opie that he went back, stood up to tough guy Hodie, and did in fact get that punch in the nose that Hodie had promised. Andy adds:

ANDY: Then it come to me that what I had been so scared of wasn't really worth being scared of a-tall. I didn't even feel that knuckle sandwich.

OPIE: You didn't?

ANDY: Not a bit. And I lit into him like a windmill in a tornado.

OPIE: What happened?

ANDY: Me and you fished that spot, didn't we?

OPIE: Yeah. Yeah!

"Opie and the Bully," Episode 33
Written by David Adler (Frank Tarloff)

When Opie starts mimicking the vagabond ways of David Browne, Andy has to get the situation under control with a talk about Opie with the wily hobo:

ANDY: There seems to be something wrong with his thinking. He's gotten a little twisted on things lately—like being able to tell the difference between right and wrong.

MR. DAVE: Oh.

ANDY: Not that that's an easy thing. Lotta grownups still struggling with that same problem. But it's especially difficult for a youngster—because things rub off on 'em so easy.

MR. DAVE: I see. Are you suggesting that I'm not fit company for Opie?

ANDY: That would seem to be the case.

MR. DAVE: Well, Sheriff, maybe I do look at things differently than other people. Is that wrong? I live by my wits. I'm not above bending the law now and then to keep clothes on my back or food in my stomach. I live the kind of life that other people would just love to live if they only had the courage. Who's to say that the boy would be happier your way or mine. Why not let him decide?

ANDY: Naww, I'm afraid it don't work that way. You can't let a young'un decide for himself. He'll grab at the first flashy thing with shiny ribbons on it. Then when he finds out there's a hook in it, it's too late. Wrong ideas come packaged with so much glitter, it's hard to convince 'em that other things might be better in the long run.

All a parent can do is say,
"Wait, trust me."
And try to keep temptation away.

"Opie's Hobo Friend," Episode 38
Written by Harvey Bullock

When moonshiner Jubal Foster's barn burns down, Andy mistakenly assumes that Opie is involved and gives him a whipping. When the truth about the fire comes out and Opie is exonerated, Andy lets Opie know that he was wrong not to have trusted his son:

ANDY: All the time I thought you didn't trust me enough to tell me the truth about that fire—turns out I was the one that didn't trust you. I apologize for that. Will you forgive me?

OPIE: Sure.

ANDY: Gooood. Police officer ought to know better than that. A person is innocent until he's proven guilty. Now, I pronounced you guilty and then went out looking for evidence. Sure am sorry about that. Glad it's over. Big load off my mind.

OPIE: Big load off my mind, too, Pa.

Andy goes on to tell a story about when he was a boy:

ANDY: Now, my pa had told me not to fool around with candles and matches and stuff like that, and when he found out about it, he indicated that I ought to give up that job. And he indicated it real good, right back there.

(Andy pats his backside.)

OPIE: Oh, did he?

ANDY: Uh-huh. Then Pa come up with an outstanding idea about how we could modernize our club. Instead of messin' around with old-fashioned and dangerous candles and matches, he suggested I change my title to…Keeper of the Flashlight.

(Andy pulls a flashlight out of a paper sack.)

ANDY: Why don't you try it. It's a lot safer.

OPIE: Gee thanks, Pa.

ANDY: It's all right.

(Andy leaves.)

OPIE (to self): He ain't so dumb.

"Keeper of the Flame," Episode 46
Written by Jack Elinson and Charles Stewart

A relaxing Sunday afternoon on the Taylors' front porch seems to Opie like a good time to discuss a small matter with his father:

OPIE: Are you in a good mood?

ANDY: Yeah, why?

OPIE: If I tell you something, would you promise not to get mad?

ANDY: Well, that all depends. What is it?

OPIE: Well, it ain't hardly worth mentionin', but I think I'd better mention it. Know that old window on Mrs. Purdy's backdoor?

ANDY: Yeah.

OPIE: Someone threw a ball and busted it.

ANDY: Would you by any chance be that someone?

(Opie nods.)

OPIE: Are you mad, Pa?

ANDY: No, no. I'm not mad. Promise you won't get mad. You won't get an allowance till that window is paid for, OK?

OPIE: OK, Pa.

Having heard the above conversation, devil-may-care visitor Ron Bailey, who has yet ever to have to pay for a broken window, pursues the topic further with Andy:

RON: Weren't you sorta rough on the kid?

ANDY: How's that?

RON: Well, why didn't you bail the little fella out?

ANDY: Bail him out?

RON: Well, yeah. It's just a window.

ANDY: Oh, oh, oh, oh, oh, oh. Yeah, yeah, I guess I could bail him out like you say. But the only trouble with that—if I was to do that, why, every time he'd get into trouble, he'd be expectin' me to come to the rescue, don't you see. This time it's a broken window, later on it'd be something bigger, and then something bigger than that. **No, he's got to learn to stand on his own two legs now. Nooo, I gotta keep that young'un straight.**

"Bailey's Bad Boy," Episode 47
Written by Leo Solomon and Ben Gershman

Opie's having a tough time understanding how to be a good sport after he finishes last in a footrace with other boys. And he's in for a tough talk from his father about his attitude, too:

ANDY: I want to talk to you. I don't think it was very nice of you to walk off the way you did.

OPIE: I didn't win. I didn't win.

ANDY: I know you didn't win, but the important thing is you was in there trying. Now that's what's important.

OPIE: They don't give you no medal for trying.

ANDY: I know that. I know they don't and it's nice to win something. It's real nice to win something. But it's more important to know how *not* to win something.

OPIE: I know how to do that real good.

ANDY: No, you don't.

OPIE: You mean there's more things I could have not won?

ANDY: I mean you could have been a nice loser. They call it sportsmanship. Now you lost this time. You try again next time. You got to learn how to take disappointment. There could be more of 'em coming up, you know. You come up smiling, you're a good loser. The other way's being a bad loser. Now what do you want to be?

OPIE: A good winner.

ANDY: Opie, we're not talking about winners. Winning ain't no problem.

It don't take courage to be a winner.

It does take courage to be a good loser.

Now you want to be a good loser—you'll be proud of your friends that did win and you'll congratulate 'em for it.

OPIE: I won't.

ANDY: You won't?

OPIE: They ain't my friends. They beat me and they got my medal.

ANDY: That's the way you feel about it? Is that the way you feel about it? Answer me?

OPIE: Yes.

ANDY: All right, fine, fine. That's the way you wanna be—as long as we understand one another. But I want you to know something, I'm disappointed in you.

Later:

OPIE: Pa, I don't want you to be disappointed in me.

(The two hug.)

ANDY: Well, you thought about what we was talking about, did you?

OPIE: Yes.

ANDY: Understand it?

OPIE: I understand some of it, I guess, but I don't understand why you're supposed to be happy about losing.

ANDY: You don't have to be happy about it. None of us are. I've lost a whole lot of times and I've been just as unhappy about it as I could be. You see, as you grow older you're going to be doing an awful lot of different kinds of things. Sometimes you'll win at 'em. Sometimes you'll lose at 'em. Now when you win, that ain't gonna be any problem to you, is it? Naw. See, we all know how to win. We grin a lot, don't we? Grin and grin and grin. But when you lose, see, that's the hard part. That's when you have to take yourself in hand, show it ain't getting you down and that you're a good sport about it, and that you're gonna try again. And when you do that, you'll be on the road to becoming a mature human being. You understand that?

OPIE: Uh-huh. I gotta try to win that race again next year. But I don't understand that part about being a mature human being.

ANDY: Well, don't you worry about that. When you are one, you'll know it. And *I sure am proud of you.*

OPIE: Thanks, Pa.

"A Medal for Opie," Episode 51
Written by David Adler (Frank Tarloff)

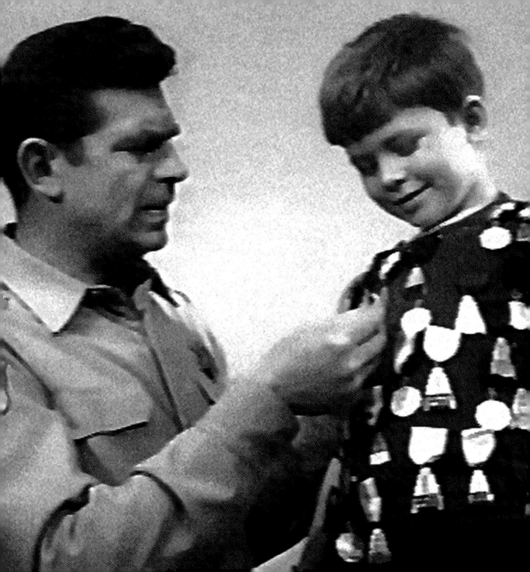

As Opie finishes brushing "again," he and Andy have a discussion about a topic even more important than tooth decay:

OPIE: Why do people get married, Pa?

ANDY: Oh, lot of reasons. To have a home, family, be together. I guess mainly because they love one another.

OPIE: Does Aunt Bee love Mr. Goss?

ANDY: Yes, she does.

OPIE: Does that mean she don't love us no more?

ANDY: No, she loves us, too.

OPIE: Kind of confusing, ain't it?

ANDY: Well, see, you can love a whole lot of people—
the more the better. You see, that's the regular kind of love,
and it's a fine, fine thing. But then you meet that special person
and you got a special love all saved up for them. That's
the marrying kind of love,
and it's the very best kind

'cause it comes from down deep inside of your heart.

OPIE: Did you and Mom have that deep down kind?

ANDY: Yes, son, we did.

"Wedding Bells for Aunt Bee," Episode 58
Written by Harvey Bullock

When Opie starts talking about a bizarre-sounding friend named Mr. McBeevee, Andy believes Opie might be letting his imagination run a little too wild—beyond just playing cowboy with his pretend horse, Blackie:

ANDY: Ope, remember the fun you was having this morning galloping around the backyard on Blackie?

(Opie nods.)

ANDY: We was both enjoying that little game. 'Course, now, the truth is there never was any real Blackie. That's just something you made up, isn't that right?

(Opie nods.)

ANDY: Now, about this Mr. McBeevee, maybe the same thing happened there. Maybe you made him up too, just for fun. And there's nothing wrong with that. What's wrong is using a Mr. McBeevee to get out of work and to explain things that seem to come from nowhere. Ope, there comes a time when you have to stop the play-acting and tell the truth. And that time's now. Right now. Ope, I want you to be man enough to tell me that Mr. McBeevee is just make-believe. That's all you have to say, and it'll all be forgotten. But if you don't, something else is gonna happen. I believe you know what I mean, don't you?

OPIE: Yes, Pa.

ANDY: All right, tell the truth. Just go ahead and say right out, "Mr. McBeevee is just make-believe." Well? Go ahead.

OPIE: Mr. McBeevee is just . . .

ANDY: Say it.

OPIE: I can't, Pa. Mr. McBeevee isn't make-believe. He's real.

ANDY: Opie . . .

OPIE: Don't you believe me, Pa, don't you?

ANDY (after a long pause and taking a deep breath): *I believe you.*

Meanwhile, downstairs, Barney and Aunt Bee are having an involved discussion about the whole situation as Andy comes down the stairs:

AUNT BEE: Andy?

ANDY: No, I didn't spank him.

BARNEY: Oh, well, that's good—just not necessary. He learned his lesson. A good talkin' to is the best thing—makin' him stay in his room.

ANDY: I didn't do that either.

BARNEY: Well, what did you do?

ANDY: I told him I believed him.

BARNEY: You told him you beli…but Andy, what he told you is impossible!

ANDY: Well, a whole lot of times I've asked him to believe things that to his mind must have seemed just as impossible.

BARNEY: Oh, but Andy, this silver hat and the jingling and the smoke from the ears—what about all that?

ANDY: Oh, I don't know, Barn. I guess it's a time like this—when you're asked to believe something that just don't seem possible—that's the moment that decides whether you've got faith in somebody or not.

BARNEY: But how can you explain it all?

ANDY: I can't.

BARNEY: But you do believe in Mr. McBeevee?

ANDY: No, no. *I do believe in Opie.*

"Mr. McBeevee," Episode 64
Written by R. Allen Saffian (Ray Allen) and Harvey Bullock

When Opie becomes worried that Andy's dating Peggy McMillan will come between him and his father, "blood brothers" pact or not, he does things to undermine their dates.

ANDY: You got yourself a peck of trouble, boy, unless you've got some mighty good reasons figured out.

OPIE: I was scared.

ANDY: Scared of what?

OPIE: Well, used to be just you and me. Then Peggy came and you always want her around now and I'm left out. And someday maybe you won't want me anymore.

ANDY: Come here a minute. I wanna tell you something, Ope, and I want you to listen real careful 'cause this is important. You're my young'un and I love you more than anything or anybody in the whole world. And nothin' or nobody can ever change that. You know, it's hard for me to tell you just how much you do mean to me 'cause you're a part of me.

OPIE: Then why do you want Peggy around so much?

ANDY: Well, because she's fun to be with and she's nice to have for a friend.

OPIE: But you got a good friend. You got Barney.

ANDY: Well, that's a little different. You may not understand this right now, but sometime you will. See, Ope, a man needs the companionship of a fine young woman. Somebody he can be with and talk to—talk about pretty things, you know. Take places—to a picture show and to a dance. Now, can you see me taking Barney to a dance? I can't take Barney to a dance. He's too short. You know, sometime I might get married again. Might not be Peggy, but it'll be somebody—somebody I like a lot, somebody I love.

But nothin' or nobody will ever change things between me and you because you're my son and we're buddies.

"Opie's Rival," Episode 73
Written by Sid Morse

Knowing that Eagle-eye Annie is Andy's prized fishing rod, Opie is surprised to learn that Andy has parted with it. When Andy lets him know that there was a good reason for doing so, Opie realizes that selling the rod was just one way of expressing which things in life are really the most important:

OPIE: Pa, it's not here.

ANDY: I know. I sold it to the mayor.

OPIE: You sold it!?

ANDY: Shhh.

OPIE: But you said you'd never sell it.

ANDY: No, not quite. I said I kept it because it gave me so much enjoyment and that I wouldn't sell it for money. And I didn't sell it for money. I just kinda swapped it for a different kind of enjoyment. So ol' Eagle-eye Annie's doin' just what she did before. Even right now, she's givin' me pleasure—real, heartwarming pleasure.

(Andy and Opie turn toward Aunt Bee, who can be heard talking on the phone with Clara about her new bed jacket.)

AUNT BEE: And do you know the color is just right for me. **I just don't know when I've ever had such a nice birthday.**

"The Bed Jacket," Episode 75
Written by Harvey Bullock and R. Allen Saffian (Ray Allen)

When a new kid on the block leads some of the young Mayberry boys into a bit of mischief, Barney once again lets Andy know how he would handle the situation:

BARNEY: I don't like it. I don't like it one bit. I tell you this is just the beginning. Goin' around breakin' street lamps. City property, mind you. Next thing you know they'll be on motorcycles and wearing them leather jackets and zoomin' around. They'll take over the whole town— a reign of terror!

ANDY: Barney, these are just boys you're talking about. They're only about eight years old.

BARNEY: Yeah, well, today's eight-year-olds are tomorrow's teenagers. I say this calls for action—and now. Nip it in the bud! First sign of youngsters goin' wrong, you got to nip it in the bud.

ANDY: I'm gonna have a talk with 'em. Now, what more you want me to do?

BARNEY: Yeah, well, just don't mollycoddle 'em. Nip it! You go read any book you want on the subject of child discipline and you'll find that every one of 'em is in favor of bud nippin'.

ANDY: I'll take care of it.

BARNEY: Only one way to take care of it.

ANDY: Nip it?

BARNEY: **In the bud.**

"One-Punch Opie," Episode 77
Written by Harvey Bullock

After a new kid in town tells Opie that he's doing too much work for his small allowance, Opie asks for a raise and then has the following exchange with Andy:

ANDY: **There are no rules for pa's and sons. It's as simple as this: each mother or father raises his boy or girl, as the case may be, the way that he thinks is best.** And I think it's best for you to get a quarter and work for it. You see when you give something, in this instance cleaning the garage, and you get something in return, like a quarter, well, that's the greatest feeling in the world. You do feel good after working, don't you?

OPIE: Uh-huh. Good and tired.

ANDY: Well, as you get bigger, why, you'll be doing more and more work for more and more return and that good feeling will get bigger. You understand what I mean?

OPIE: I think so.

ANDY: Good.

OPIE: I'm not gonna get the seventy-five cents?

ANDY: Right.

OPIE: And I'm gonna have to work for the twenty-five cents.

ANDY: Right. All clear to you?

OPIE: Yeah. The bigger you get, the tireder you get.

ANDY: Well, you just think about that for a while.

OPIE: Do I have to?

ANDY: Don't you want to think about it?

OPIE: It makes me kinda sad.

ANDY: Well, the thing to do when you're feeling sad is to shoot for the good feeling.

OPIE: Cleaning the garage?

ANDY: Right.

And soon, after Andy and Opie have another father-and-son talk, it's time for Barney to chime in again with more fathering advice for Andy:

BARNEY: Kids, what do they know about life, huh?

ANDY: Well, I'll tell you one thing—a whole lot more than we give 'em credit for.

BARNEY: Yeah, that's true. But they need guidance.

ANDY: Yeah, that's true.

BARNEY: And this time you really muffed it.

ANDY: How's that?

BARNEY: Well, not being emotionally involved with the child, I think I can be pretty doggone objective.

ANDY: Oh, you been at the magazine section of the Sunday paper again, ain't you?

BARNEY: I skim through it.

ANDY: And, uh, on the subject of child rearing, it said?

BARNEY: There's a definite trend toward stronger discipline.

ANDY: Like what?

BARNEY: Like a good clout once in a while.

ANDY: Oh, come on.

BARNEY: Well, Andy, have you ever known the magazine section of the Sunday paper to lie?

ANDY: Did your father ever hit you?

BARNEY: Well, he couldn't. I was a lot bigger than he was.

ANDY: I thought as a child you were sickly.

BARNEY: Well, he was sicklier. Now, Andy, the way I'd talk to a son of mine . . .

ANDY: Wait a minute, wait a minute, wait a minute, wait a minute. Just don't start off on that imaginary child of yours again.

BARNEY: Look, Andy, I'm . . .

ANDY: All the theories in the world don't mean a thing until you got a child of your own. There ain't no use talking about it **'cause you don't know what you're gonna do until you're faced with it.**

"Opie and the Spoiled Kid," Episode 84
Written by Jim Fritzell and Everett Greenbaum

When Opie, who earlier had been out playing with his new slingshot, dashes away from the dinner table and runs to his bedroom just after Andy tells about having found a dead song-bird in the yard, Andy knows what must have happened and has a talk with Opie:

ANDY: You killed that bird, didn't you?

(Opie can't answer.)

ANDY: Didn't you?

(Opie gulps and then nods slowly.)

ANDY: Remember me telling you to be careful with this thing?

OPIE: I'm sorry, Pa.

ANDY: That won't bring that bird back to life. Being sorry is not the magic word that makes everything right again.

OPIE: You gonna give me a whippin'?

ANDY: No…I'm not gonna give you a whippin'.

(Andy walks over and raises the window.)

ANDY: Do you hear that? That's those young birds chirping for their mama that's never coming back. Now, you just listen to that for a while.

Opie shows that he has done some listening and has taken his father's words to heart:

OPIE: I got to thinkin' last night that since their ma ain't comin' back and since it's my fault and since just bein' sorry won't help, I'm gonna take over and feed 'em.

ANDY: Oh, you are?

OPIE: Uh-huh. And Pa, there's three of 'em. I call 'em Winken, Blinken, and Nod.

ANDY: Them's fine bird names.

OPIE: But Pa, I'm kinda worried. I never tried to take care of birds before.

ANDY: Well, I don't know much about raisin' birds either. I reckon you just feed 'em till they get big and strong enough to fly off and take care of themselves.

(Aunt Bee comes out the on the porch.)

AUNT BEE: Breakfast, everybody!

OPIE: I can't come in right now, Aunt Bee. I just can't!

ANDY (preparing to leave): Come in quick as you can.

AUNT BEE (to Andy): Why is Opie acting so strange?

ANDY: Well, the boy's facing up to some awful unusual problems. Fact is,

Opie's just become a mother.

As a good father, Andy helps Opie fulfill his efforts as a mother:

ANDY: Well, Ope, I know how fond you are of 'em. And I don't reckon it'd hurt for them to stay around a while longer, but 'member, we did talk about one day you was goin' have to turn 'em loose…and the longer you put it off, why, the worse it's gonna get.

OPIE: But I can't, Pa…I just can't!

ANDY: Well, you remember you took over this job 'cause they lost their ma. Well, there's that one other thing that she would've done—that's to let 'em go, let 'em be on their own, be free like they's intended to be.

OPIE: But what if they can't fly away? Maybe I didn't do all the right things. I mean account of I wasn't really their ma.

ANDY: No, you did all the right things. I expect they'll be able to fly.

OPIE: 'Course, Pa, if they can't fly away, then I could keep them as pets, couldn't I? They could live right here, couldn't they? . . . But they don't wanna be pets. They're supposed to fly away like you said.

(Opie takes the cage down, opens the door, and watches with glee as each bird successfully flies away from his hands.)

OPIE: They're OK, Pa! They all flew off OK. Guess, I did good job, huh, Pa?

ANDY: You sure did, son.

OPIE: **Cage sure looks awful empty, don't it, Pa?**

ANDY: **Yes, son, it sure does. But don't the trees seem nice and full?**

"Opie the Birdman," Episode 96
Written by Harvey Bullock

After Opie learns the identity of the man whose money he found, Opie breaks open his piggybank of savings. Thinking that he's on a spending spree, Andy catches up with Opie back at the same store where earlier he had purchased a new fishing rod:

ANDY: Opie, I'm mad and I think you know what I'm mad about, don't you?

OPIE: Well, I guess you're mad because I broke the bank.

ANDY: That's part of it. Ever hear of a man named Parnell Rigsby?

OPIE: You know about him?

ANDY: Yeah. He was in here this afternoon, wasn't he? And when he told you that he was the one that lost the money, you just stood there and didn't say a word about it, didn't you? And even after he told you he was the one that lost it, you went straight out to spend some more money, didn't you?

OPIE: But I wasn't buying anything at the store, Pa.

ANDY: What?

OPIE: I was getting my ten dollars back for the fishing rod.

(Opie reaches in his pocket to get the money to give to Andy.)

OPIE: Fifty dollars. It's all there.

ANDY: **Well, I did it again, didn't I?**

OPIE: **Did what, Pa?**

ANDY: **Oh, not realizing . . . you're really something, you know that, Ope?**

"Opie's Fortune," Episode 136
Written by Ben Joelson and Art Baer

ANDY: **If you're selling something, the buyer's got a right to know everything that's wrong with it. Otherwise, it's not quite honest.**

After Andy teaches Opie a lesson on honesty when selling his bike, Opie uses the same policy of full disclosure inadvertently to sink Barney's effort to sell the Taylors' house. Andy suspects that Opie is just getting back at him for ruining his bike sale. But, actually, Opie is just doing exactly what Andy had taught him earlier:

OPIE: I was thinking about what you said.

ANDY: What?

OPIE: **That if you're selling something, you should tell people the truth about it or else it ain't honest.** That don't just go for bikes, does it, Pa? It goes for houses, too, don't it?

ANDY: Oh. Well, uh, Opie, the fact is…bikes are bikes and houses are houses. You understand?

OPIE: No, Pa.

ANDY: Well, maybe I can, uh, clear it up for you. When I bought this house from Old Man Parmaley, the crack was already in the ceiling of the kitchen and Mr. Parmaley had just painted the kitchen.

OPIE: So it wouldn't show?

ANDY: That's right. And when Mr. Parmaley bought the house, there were probably things wrong with it at that time and he wasn't told either, so he just passed it on to me. Now, that's the way it is, Ope. That's the way it is and that's the way it always has been.

OPIE: You mean that kids should be honest, but the grownups don't have to be?

ANDY: Uh, no, no. No, it's not that. It's just like I said, uh, bikes are bikes and houses are houses. You better go to bed.

"Barney Fife, Realtor," Episode 143
Written by Bill Idelson and Sam Bobrick

Andy had been proud that Opie won when competing with another boy for a job at the grocery store, but that's just the beginning:

ANDY: How was work today?

    OPIE: There's something I've gotta tell you, Pa.

ANDY: I'm listening.

    OPIE: I'm not working there anymore.

ANDY: That's what I heard.

    OPIE: Huh?

ANDY: I don't know what to think of you, you know that? I wouldn't feel so bad if you hadn't got the job to start with, but you got fired. I was never fired in my life. And on top of everything else, I had to make a fool out of myself bragging on you in front of Floyd and Goober and everybody.

OPIE: I had to get fired, Pa, because …

ANDY: You had to get fired? You had to get fired, so you could play baseball. What are you doing here anyway? Game get called off?

OPIE: There was no game.

ANDY: There was no game?

OPIE: I just made that up.

ANDY: What are you talking about?

OPIE: I didn't mean to tell a lie, Pa, but I had to.

ANDY: Opie, I don't believe I know what you're talk-ing about at all. You sound like you meant to get yourself fired. And I want you to tell me the truth.

OPIE: You see, this other boy, Billy …

ANDY: Yes.

OPIE: He wanted the job to pay some bills. His Pa's been sick. They've got some bills.

ANDY: I'm sorry.

OPIE: That's OK.

ANDY: You know, when I was bragging on you to Floyd and Goober,

I told 'em how proud I was to have a boy like you.

But that's not quite true. You're a man.

"Opie's Job," Episode 160
Written by Art Baer and Ben Joelson

When it comes time for Opie's first school dance, Andy tries to find the right way to say to the shy Opie, "I hope you dance":

ANDY: Let me put it another way. The sign that a fella is growing up is when he can change his mind and do something that he thought he didn't want to do, but that he knows he really should do. Do you follow me?

OPIE: Yeah, you're forcing me to go.

ANDY: I'm not!

OPIE: Then if it isn't forcing, Pa, what is it?

ANDY: Well, uh, it, uh, well, I know that you're gonna be glad that I suggested that you go.

OPIE: What if I still don't want to?

ANDY: Well, how it would be in a case like that is that I'd have to suggest a little harder.

OPIE: But…

ANDY: I want you to go.

OPIE: Why, Pa?

ANDY: Because I just want you to go.

OPIE: Yes sir.

ANDY: **Ope, every time a fella faces a hurdle and he's afraid to jump it, but he goes ahead and he jumps it anyway, he finds out it wasn't much of a jump after all.**

A little later:

ANDY: Opie, I want you to understand. There's a big difference between forcing and suggesting because there's just a big difference and…someday when you grow up and have children of your own, I'd like to be around when you explain it to your boy.

"Look Paw, I'm Dancing," Episode 181
Written by Ben Starr

When Opie starts asking lots of questions about babies, it's time for Andy to have a talk with Opie about the facts of life:

GOOBER: Andy, I wouldn't waste no time tellin' him.

ANDY: I won't, Goob. I'll tell him, but there's a proper time and place for everything.

GOOBER: I remember when Daddy told me about it. He used the birds and the bees as an example.

ANDY: Don't you think that's a little outdated?

GOOBER: 'Course, you could always tell him about the mackerel swimming downstream.

ANDY: That's salmon, Goob. And they swim upstream.

GOOBER: As long as he learns the reason they're swimming.

After Andy has that talk with Opie about finding babies and where they come from, Opie gives a briefing to his pal Arnold:

ARNOLD: What took you so long? Your pa bawl you out?

OPIE: No, he sat me down and gave me a talk about the facts of life.

ARNOLD: Did you tell him you knew all about it?

OPIE: No, **I didn't want to spoil it for him.**

"Opie Finds a Baby," Episode 199
Written by Stan Dreben and Sid Mandel

Opie's too excited to eat his breakfast:

OPIE: I'm all ready!

    ANDY: What do you mean you're all ready? You barely touched your breakfast.

OPIE: Well, I don't think I ought to eat too much with a long hike ahead of me.

    ANDY: Eat!

    AUNT BEE: That's when you need it most, Opie—when you're burning up your vitamins.

OPIE: But I'm just not very hungry, Pa.

    ANDY: The only excuse for not eating at mealtimes is when you're sick.

OPIE: Well, I'm not sick, but gee, Pa . . .

    ANDY: We don't waste food around here. When something's served to you, you eat it.

Now, there's a lot of people in this world who would give anything to sit down to a meal like that, so you go ahead.

Later, Andy is way too full to eat more spaghetti after two previous meals, but Opie makes sure that Andy practices what he earlier preached:

OPIE: You mean you're gonna leave all that food on your plate, Pa?

    ANDY: Well, uh.

OPIE: What about what you told me this morning?

    ANDY: What was that?

OPIE: You know, about all the people in the world not having enough to eat and how it's almost a crime for us not to finish everything on our plate.

    ANDY: Well, Ope, there are extenuating circumstances.

OPIE: I even told our scoutmaster what you said and he said that if more people felt that way, it would be a better world.

    ANDY: He's a fine man.

OPIE: If this food weren't here, it might be in India. So we should eat it and not let it go to waste.

    ANDY: Well, Ope…

    HELEN: Eat!

"Dinner at Eight," Episode 206
Written by Budd Grossman

Opie wants to punt his piano lessons when he finds out that his football practice is scheduled for the same time that he's supposed to be practicing the piano:

ANDY: It was wrong and you know it was wrong. Now you promised to practice that piano two hours every afternoon.

OPIE: But how did I know that Flip Conroy was going to coach us? He's one of the biggest professional football players.

AUNT BEE: He did have a rather difficult choice, Andy.

ANDY: People have difficult choices their whole lives and they've got to learn to make the right ones. I knew I was gonna wind up forcing him to practice. Opie, when you start something, you have got to finish it.

OPIE: I started playing football long before I started taking piano lessons.

ANDY: That's got nothing to do with anything. Now you made up your own mind that you wanted to take piano lessons, right?

OPIE: Yes, Pa.

ANDY: So you're taking 'em. And you said you wanted to be good at it and to be good at anything you've got to give it your all.

OPIE: But I want to be good at football too, and Mr. Conroy said I have to give *that* my all.

ANDY: There are more important things than football.

OPIE: But Pa.

ANDY: And you can't do two things at the same time and do 'em well. So, you will be practicing that piano every afternoon from 3:30 to 5:30. Do you understand?

OPIE: Yes, Pa.

The doorbell rings, Flip Conroy enters the house, and, after some discussion, he plays the piano and demonstrates that someone can indeed master more than one skill at a time. After Flip finishes playing, Andy speaks again:

ANDY: **Well, there's a lot of different ways of figuring things.**

"Opie's Piano Lesson," Episode 215
Written by Leo and Pauline Townsend

Father knows best?:

ANDY: **No thirteen-year-old boy will do hard labor on a Saturday afternoon unless he's buttering up his folks. It's an unwritten law.**

Maybe Opie's cleaning out the garage in order to rehearse a new rock 'n' roll band with Clifford and the boys. Playing in a band is fine until Opie starts slacking off on his homework, not coming home until late at night, and worrying Andy and Aunt Bee:

OPIE (coming in the front door): Hi, Pa. Hi, Aunt Bee.

ANDY: Where have you been?

OPIE: At the gig, Pa.

ANDY: I called there over an hour ago and you were gone.

OPIE: Well, we got another gig and we all went over to Clifford's house to decide what we're gonna play.

ANDY: Did it ever occur to you that we might be worried about where you were?

OPIE: Well, Pa, I'm not a little kid anymore. Even Clifford says so.

ANDY: Clifford?

OPIE: That's right.

ANDY: I see.

OPIE: You can probably tell how I'm a little older by the way I'm not arguing or anything.

AUNT BEE: Opie, the fact remains that you did come in late.

OPIE: Aunt Bee, late for a kid and late for an older person comes at two different times.

AUNT BEE: Opie!

ANDY: Go to bed.

OPIE: OK.

(Opie goes upstairs.)

ANDY: He leaves here at five o'clock a kid and he comes back seven hours later and he's grown up. I don't understand that.

Andy and Aunt Bee continue their discussion about what to do about Opie's forsaking all other responsibilities for his music:

AUNT BEE: It's that boy Clifford, you know.

ANDY: Nope. He might have sparked it, but Opie's got a mind of his own. He should know better.

AUNT BEE: Well, he doesn't seem to. And I think you should discipline him.

ANDY: I don't think that's the way to handle it either. He'd just think I was keeping him from doing something that was important to him. Remember I said he's a teenager now? I'll just let him go till he gets in just enough trouble, and then he'll find out something.

AUNT BEE: Well, I never heard of such a thing!

When Clara intervenes, at Aunt Bee's request, with some sound advice for Opie, Andy learns a new tune as well:

ANDY:
Clara, sometimes a parent can't see what he should do, and sometimes it takes a person from the outside to show him.

And I'd like to thank you.

CLARA: Groovy!

"Opie's Group," Episode 228
Written by Doug Tibbles

FLOYD: That Opie is a fine boy.

GOOBER: Yeah, a nice relationship between Andy and Opie.

FLOYD: Yeah, *father and son.*

"Opie's Job," Episode 160
Written by Art Baer and Ben Joelson